reading and writing

Shirley Clarke & Barry Silsby

Illustrated by Marida Hines

BROCKHAMPTON PRESS
LONDON

Make a regular time to read together when you are both relaxed. Just before bedtime is a good time.

Let your child choose the book. It will often be an old favourite.

Encourage this as it is an important stage in reading to hear the same story many times.

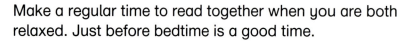

Settle down somewhere quiet and comfortable.

You, the parent, should begin reading. At first you will be doing all the reading.

After a while, particularly after hearing the same story several times, your child will begin to join in. At first, this will be only in certain places (like 'Fee Fi Fo Fum' in Jack and the Beanstalk), but later it could be the whole book.

Continue reading together until your child stops or indicates that he or she wishes to read alone. Be ready to join in again if he or she tires or has any difficulty with words.

Always tell your child the words he or she is having difficulty with immediately so that the flow of the story is maintained.

Even when your child is a good reader, he or she will enjoy this sort of experience.

NOTES FOR PARENTS

Research has shown that when children and parents work together at home, the child's work at school improves.

The purpose of the *Headstart* books is to provide activities which your child will enjoy doing and which will encourage learning to take place in the home.

To become a good reader and writer, your child needs, above all, to be confident. Always encourage your child's efforts, no matter how basic they might seem to you. Always bear the following points in mind:

- Children begin writing by making arbitrary marks. Soon, recognisable letters and numbers appear, followed by spaces and some recognisable words. Enthuse over your child's writing, whatever it looks like. The acid test is whether your child can 'read' his or her writing to you, not whether you can read it.

- An early insistence on correct spelling often causes a writing block in children. Children often say, 'I can't write.' What they mean is, 'I can't spell.' If your child says this, try the following strategies:

  (a) Say, 'It doesn't matter as long as you know what it says. Put what you think.'
  (b) Say, 'Try putting the beginning letter or the letters you do know in the word. We can put the rest in when you've finished.'

  The important thing is to encourage a flow of writing. If all else fails, write the word yourself. (There are activities in this book which will help your child's spelling, and another book in the series, 'Spelling', deals exclusively with spelling.)

- Talk with your child about the activities, and about his or her writing. Discussion will improve the quality and quantity of the writing.

The activities on pp. 16–17, 20–21 and 22–23 of this book are particularly designed to help your child enjoy the process of writing.

Information about some of the other activities in this book:

Pages 10–11   What is it?

All of the words the child needs to complete the labels are on the two pages. Afterwards, discuss other labels he or she could use.

Pages 14–15   Sounds right

Children often find it difficult to isolate the first sound of a word. If your child has difficulty with this activity, encourage him or her to say the first word with each of the others (cat/pig, cat/cow, cat/sheep, etc). This should make it easier for him or her to identify the two that begin in the same way.

Pages 18–19   Looks right

It is not necessary for your child to be able to read the words in order to do the activity. If he or she has difficulty, try getting him or her to compare the first word with the others, letter by letter.

This is my book

My name is _____

I live at _____

_____

_____

_____

The members of my family are called

_____

_____

_____

_____

Draw a picture of yourself here.

I have _____ hair and _____ eyes.

I am _____ years old.

My favourite colour is _____ .

One to one

Can you find the birds which look the same?

Join them together with a line.

Now join the words which are the same, in the same way.

a

school

name

and

girl

girl

a

the

name

boy

the

school

boy

they

and

they

9

What is it?

Some of the words have been left out in this picture.

Can you put them back in?

eye

mouth

ear

leg

nose

hair

arm

foot

Try putting on some other labels of your own.

11

What comes next?

The last item in each row is missing.

Can you say what comes next?

Draw and colour the last item in each row.

12

p b p b p b p

n m n m n m n

u y u y u y

s z s z s z s z

Sounds right

Look at the first picture in each row.

Say the word and listen to the sound it begins with.

Put a ring round one picture in the row that begins with the same sound.

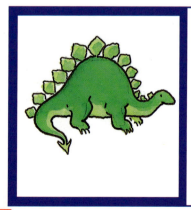   

15

Conversations

Look at these pictures.

What do you think the children are saying?

Think carefully, then write what you think in the speech bubbles. (You can get someone to help you write if you want to.)

Looks right

Look carefully at the word on the red balloon in each row.

Now put a ring round the yellow balloon which has the same word on it.

boy

big

baby

boy

mummy

daddy

mummy

granny

the

they

the

then

What happens next?

Look at this picture story carefully.

How do you think the story will end?

Draw or write what you think happened next.

My own story

These pages are for your own story. Think about the story first.

Who will be in it?   How will it start?   What will happen?

How will it end?   Draw a picture from your story here.

Look at your picture and remember your story.

Now write your story here.

Continue on a piece of paper if you need more space.

Look carefully at the borders.

Can you finish colouring them?

Odd one out

One picture in each row is different.

Put a ring round the odd one out.

a g a a

n n n h

b b d b

British Library Cataloguing in Publication Data
Clarke, Shirley
  Headstart: reading and writing: 5–7.–(Headstart)
  I. Title II. Silsby, Barry III. Series
  372.4

ISBN 1-86019-518-0
First published 1991

This edition published 1997 by Brockhampton
Press, a member of Hodder Headline PLC Group.
10 9 8 7 6 5 4 3
1999 1998 1997

Typeset by Oxprint, Oxford OX2 6TR.

Printed in India.